Real Estate Hacks

First-Time Homebuyers Should Know

Breaking Down The Process For First-Time Homebuyers

By Aundrea Beach-Greco, CMPS

Copyright © 2019 Aundrea Beach-Greco

All rights reserved.

ISBN: 9781796620917

DEDICATION

This is dedicated to my daughter Gianna,
who has shown me that life has no boundaries
and to keep dreaming BIG!

CONTENTS

	Acknowledgments	i
1	Owning Vs Renting	1
2	Needs and Desires	9
3	Getting Your First Home Loan	14
4	Programs For First-time Homebuyers	22
5	14 Common Mistakes First Timers Make	28
6	12 Steps To Buying Your Home	44
7	To Hire a Real Estate Agent or Not To Hire a Real Estate Agent	53
8	What You Need To Know About Home Inspections	65
9	The Closing Process	73
10	Moving Tips	81
11	Horror Stories in Real Estate	88

ACKNOWLEDGMENTS

Thank you to my husband Louis Buddy Greco and my daughter Gianna Greco. This book would not have been possible without the support and encouragement from them. Words cannot express my gratitude.

Chapter 1
Owning vs. Renting

At some point your family and friends will encourage you to buy a home. Wondering if it's the right thing to do is completely normal. The more you know about it and the process will help ease those fears. Owning a home provides a sense of security, satisfaction, contentment and fulfilment that you can't get from renting.

Americans seem to find out that there is nothing sweeter in life than buying and owning their own real estate. The American Dream is to have a home of your own, right?

Pride of ownership is the number one reason people year to own a home. It means you can paint, decorate, turn up your music, and make it your own. Homeownership gives you and your family a sense of security and stability plus making it an investment in your future.

However, owning a home is a lifetime investment, so proper preparation and financial management practices are required when buying a home. Besides the funds that are involves in this investment, there are other commitments, such as attention and time.

There are so many benefits of owning a home, including how it gives you prestige and peace of mind. Some of the main reasons why you would want have your own home:

It is Cheaper to buy a House than to Rent One in the Long Run

Although buying a house is more expensive at the outset, it can actually be cheaper than renting in the long term if you play your cards right. Rents are rising in most part of the country and by owning you can lock in your monthly payment. So by paying more upfront on your own home, you can actually save money in the long run.

House prices tend to rise over time, so a house is one of the best investments you can make. Home prices in the U.S. have risen 3% to 6% a year for the past 20 years. That trend is likely to continue. So if you buy a home now, you've put your capital in a safe investment where it is likely to grow. In time, as the interest rate decreases, you will discover that the interest you pay is lower than what you would have paid for if you had opted for a rent.

Having a roof over your head is important and necessary, so why not own your own home and build equity instead of helping your landlord become rich off you.

Equity is Built Every Month on the House

Equity is the amount the home is worth minus any loans you have against the property. So for instance if you buy a home and it's worth $200,000 but you owe $175,000 then the equity you have is $25,000. As you make mortgage payments every month, there is always a reduction in the amount being owed.

This reduction you experience in your mortgage each month boosts your equity. It is usually the lowest during the first payment, and highest at the last payment. Therefore, your equity increases as each month and each year passes by.

Mortgage Rates are Low

Interest rates are currently very low. This makes it relatively inexpensive to take out a mortgage. The lower the interest rate, the less you actually pay for your house and the sooner you can pay the mortgage off.

When you can put a down payment down on a home and pay equal or less than you pay in rent then there is definitely a benefit. Why wouldn't you own a home if it was equivalent to renting?

Even a few years ago, when it was more expensive it still makes more sense to buy a home rather than rent.

You Enjoy an Exclusion of Capital Gains

You will get to enjoy this great benefit of capital gains exclusion when you go to sell your home but only after you have lived in the home as your primary residence for two of the last five years.

When the house is sold after your 2 years of living there, the profits of $250,000 if you're single, or $500,00 if you're married, can be realized tax free without owing any taxes related to those capital gains.

This may sound weird now when you haven't even bought a home, but trust me it will be important later. The worth of your home will increase over time and in the future when you go to sell it, that's when you will enjoy the benefit of capital gains tax.

Homeowners Enjoy a Different Standard of Living

There is always a feeling of accomplishment when you have your own home. This feeling comes with a sense of freedom and independence.

The home you live in definitely belongs to you, you can do whatever you want and you have full control over the house. You do not feel daunted of increases in rent costs, or the risks of being kicked out of the house, and you are free to make improvements and changes as you wish.

Also, owning your home gives your children the guarantee of attending good schools without any quick notice from the landlord to vacate your rented house or apartment due to any reasons.

There is a Great Tax Benefit Enjoyed by Homeowners

There are significant tax benefits associated with buying a home from the time you purchase it and even on a continuous basis.

You enjoy your benefit the same year you acquire your home – loan costs and discount points can be claimed on your taxes, no matter who paid them. Whatso I mean by points? Mortgage points are generally of two types: discount points and origination points. Each of these points is a percentage of the amount your borrow.

Discount points involve prepaid interest, are deductible tax-wise and can reduce your total mortgage payment. While origination points are not deductible tax-wise, they can be negotiated, and are not always required. Origination points also compensate lenders.

Every year you can minus the interest paid you paid on the mortgage from your taxable income. Great savings can be achieved through this especially at the initial stage of your mortgage.

In the beginning, the bulk of your monthly payments is made up of interest that you can write off. As you pay on your mortgage and time passes the amount of interest you pay will lessen and lessen.

Any Maintenance or Improvement Made is for Your Own Good

Once you buy a home, you are not restricted by anyone (other than the HOA) with regards any improvements or maintenance you want to perform. It is your property and you can change whatever you'd like.

You'll be able to redecorate and renovate any way you like, any time you like. Rules about the paint colors you can use will be a thing of the past. And you'll be able to tear out walls, install a powder room and make any other improvements you want. Best of all, if you decide to sell, you'll recoup at least part of the cost of the improvements.

If you're a renter, you only enjoy any improvement in your rented house for as long as you stay there. Once you leave, the homeowner benefits from the improvements.

There are so many other benefits to owning a home such as feeling more secure, your kids will have a safe haven to call their own, you can have pets, you'll be more involved in your community and you'll have a legacy to leave your family.

Some Negatives of Owning

We know that owning a home is not always sunshine and rainbows, so here is a list of the disadvantages that come with owning a home:

- Costs. It takes hard work and effort to save money for a down payment and buy a home. You may not be eligible for down payment assistance, you may not have a family member to help you, so planning to buy a home must be thought out. It may

not be within your budget and you may not be able to save any extra money for the extra costs involved in buying and owning a home.
- You are responsible for all the repairs and maintenance. When you rent the leases specify that the owner is responsible for making repairs, but when you own your own home, you need to make sure you save some extra money set aside for when something breaks. And sadly there is no way around that. However, with the right strategy and a little positive thinking, maintenance can even be fun.
- Job insecurity. The mortgage payments will be due every month and if it's paid late you risk hurting your credit. If you have an unstable job or career, it might not be good time for you to buy a home, since without income it might be difficult to make the mortgage payments and keep the house.
- A Travelling Job. Owning a house will definitely give you roots and a sense of family security, but it also means you are tied to one location. If you have a job that requires a lot of travel, owning may not be for you.

The Negative Aspects of Renting

- The monthly rent you pay goes to the landlord. It represents the fee you pay for using their property and it will never amount to an investment, as no matter how long you stay there. The paid rent will not earn you property rights or ownership status.
- All the structural and decorative home improvements you make will have to stay behind when you move to a different place. Additionally, you might also need approval for any desired major redecoration. We all like to decorate and improve our homes, however, if you are renting, you should definitely consider the cost-value of the desired modifications and if they are worth it in the long run.
- Renting does not build your equity. While your monthly mortgage payment is based on a principal and interest, the

principal adds up to your initial down payment to increase your true ownership of the place and build you equity. That does not happen with renting, where the entire payment is not an investment, but just a fee for using that place.
- Renting is unfortunately not an investment, but part your increased living cost. Rent payments have no investment components.
- You have no control over your rent, something that can make long-term budgeting very difficult. As the rent amount might fluctuate, this is a big part of your budget and your living costs that can cause major changes in your life.
- Renting lacks the permanence and sense of security that a family has when having a place to call their own.
- It does not always give you the freedom to smoke inside premises, make home improvements or even have pets.
- Renting is not always cheaper! Considering the investment and the equity aspect of a mortgage, as well as the increase in rent prices and moving costs, rent can actually turn out to be more expensive than buying.

While this might be a continuing, never ending debate, there are a number of hidden, amazing benefits that only owning a home can provide.

We've already mentioned most benefits, but here are the biggest factors that drive people to home ownership.

- Your savings are not subject to inflation, and neither is your mortgage payments! If you opt for a fixed payment mortgage, both the price of your house as well as your payments will be locked to a fixed sum for the next 15 to 25 years. That means that no matter the inflation, you will continue to pay your normal monthly mortgage rate and at the end of the mortgage period, own a beautiful, exquisite home for you and your family to enjoy.
- It is a great investment. Once you buy a home, the price of the house is fixed to that specific amount, which means that the

- credit and mortgage payments will stay the same no matter how much the value of your home increases.
- What a great legacy! There can be nothing better than leaving a home behind, as a legacy for your kids. An investment in a home can also mean an investment in the future of your children.

There is a lot to consider when you want to buy a home.

Getting from renting to homeownership is a highly challenging, but an exciting and amazing decision to make.

And no matter what people say, owning a house is the first step to make in giving ourselves the home we've been dreaming of. Because, at the end of the day, as we all know, there is no place like home.

Chapter 2
Needs and Desires

Imagine what your dream house looks like. You have particular wants and needs and you can't imagine not having them fulfilled. But there are some desires you may have to forgo due to affordability issues.

There are numerous things to be considered when buying a home.

> Is there a certain are you want to live in?
>
> A certain school district for your children?
>
> Would you like a swimming pool?
>
> What can you afford and what is your budget?

Budgeting restricts us more than anything else in most cases when buying a home. While some things are necessary for any home, others will just stay on the wish list without ever coming to reality.

Before starting your house hunt for a new home, it is advisable to make a list of all your basic needs and desires while targeting the most important ones.

Making a list and highlighting what truly matters is the way to go. On top of it all it will make your house hunt easier, knowing you can get most of your need list items and try for the dream list items., however having a complete list can be complicated.

Buying a house involves a lot of moving parts. Think about budget, location, having financing in place before going out to look at homes and finding a good real estate agent.

You also need to be aware of the traps and scams out there for new home buyers.

After making your list, you may find your wants and desires may change from when you started the process. Some criteria may be

- Distance from your job
- Schools for your children
- Nearby stores & shopping
- Pool
- Amenities

Each of us have different needs and requirements, depending upon your personality. Basic needs cannot be ignored or compromised. Desires on the other hand, are left on the wish list for later on. You need to make a clear distinction between your needs and desires. You can work on the wish list on a later date.

Without being limited by a certain budget and the basic requirements that you can't let go of, you should be able to find a great home at an affordable price.

Pet Owners

The majority of people have pets and think of them as members of the family. Some people openly confess that their children and pets are almost equals.

Pets have so much importance in the lives of some people, and we have adopted a lifestyle to include our pets in everything we do.

It is essential to discover if the neighborhood you're seeking has any pet retractions before you buy. If you are a pet lover, a fenced space and yard is important for your pet and their security.

If you are a pet lover, you may prefer tile or hardwood floors and the homes' layout is super important to accommodate your pets.

Traffic in the area may be another concern because certain pets go outdoors if doors are left open and if there is heavy traffic in the area then it would be a problem.

You may want to see if your neighbors are pet-friendly since it will create a happier environment for you and your pet.

You'll probably want to see how far the needed pet services are away from your new home community, such as the vet and groomer – how far are they to your new home.

Location

Remember that old saying Location – Location – Location? Well, it is one of the most significant decisions when buying a home. You can always change features and things inside a home but you can never change its location.

Location influences your life everyday.

A home represents peace and happiness so the place that you choose for your home must be a comfortable distance from your work and close to friends and relatives.

The home's price can be based on location and the conditions of the property. When someone starts looking for their house, it is important to consider location and how far the home is from schools, shopping and other facilities.

Location may cost you in price today when buying your home, however it may save you later on from other expenses and headaches. Location can make or break your ability to resell the home in the future for top dollar.

Home means many things to people but it is your sanctuary so choose it wisely with the best location you can to meet your needs and budget.

Schools

If you have children or are planning to have children, having nearby schools is undoubtably an important consideration when buying a home.

Living in an area with good public schools or nearby private schools may sway your buying decisions. Being close to the schools will also contribute to your peace of mind and lessen your commute times.

Even if you don't have kids yet, it's a good idea to have quality neighborhood schools nearby as to increase the value of your investment so it's important to make sure they are close by when selecting a home.

If you are having difficulty finding a home in your desires school district and price range, then you may need to rethink your requirements and find another home that meets your criteria.

Neighborhood

Different neighborhoods and communities will have different characteristics. Sometimes, the neighborhood becomes a reason for your decision and sways where you buy and sometimes a neighborhood is a reason you move away.

You must make sure you are in a neighborhood that offers the closest possible match to your wants and needs list and the kind of lifestyle you live.

Don't choose the wrong neighborhood thinking it will work out for you later on, it usually doesn't.

That leads to your neighbors. You can't usually pick your neighbors and that can make or a wonderful community or a horrible one. Good neighbors watch over the neighborhood and over you and your kids and your pets.

A good neighborhood is not only a blessing, but is a fundamental need, because without it there is no peace in your home.

Neighborhood is one of those items on your needs and desire list and may have to be compromised depending upon budget, however this should be at the top of your needs list.

Chapter 3
Getting Your First Home Loan

Starting into the housing market can be intimidating for anyone. Ever since the housing market crashed in 2007, the road to recovery has been rather uneven.

This includes buyers being held back due to increasingly stricter standards for lending. However, things have been turning around slowly, with markets showing slight signs of improvement.

For starters, banks have finally begun to goa little easy on the minimum requirements, and with lender who are offering mortgages and down payments at the rate of a mere 3%, this may just be a good time to consider jumping into the market.

With the housing market heating up and consumers all ready to but a home, it is time that you begin to prepare for the road that lies ahead of you.

Understanding the Importance of a Good Credit Score

One of the most important factors that will decide the interest that you will end up paying on your mortgage is your credit health.

In fact, its impact is so significant that the difference could be in the range of thousands of dollars – based on nothing but your credit score. Let us give you a small example to make this a little clearer.

Let us take $178,500, which is the median home value in the United States, as the amount in question.

Pretend that 2 people want a 30-year fixed mortgage each for their respective $178,500 homes and they are paying the same amounts as down payment.

The difference between them is that while one has a poor credit score of 620, the other comes with an excellent score that is 760.

In almost every case, the one with a poor credit score will end up paying more- even a 3.5 and 5 percent interest rate difference could mean $59,000 or more over a mortgage's lifetime.

Thus, this should be enough of an indication to tell you why having a good credit score before you take on a mortgage is an important factor.

So what can you do to ensure that your credit is in good shape before you jump into the mortgage market? Here is a short guide to help you in doing just that.

#1. Monitor and analyze your credit history.

- With your credit score being such a crucial aspect of the final approval, not going into the process blindly is obviously a good thing to do.
- Keep a tab on your score well in advance – this will help you to have an accurate estimate of the rate that you can expect, and if your credit score is good enough, it will help you get approval.

- Also, take this opportunity to find out areas where your credit history requires improvement, and take steps to measure the improvement that takes place.

#2. Report errors and inconsistencies.

- A study by the Federal Trade Commission in the year 2013 stated that 1 out of every 4 consumers found such errors in their credit reports that significantly affected their credit scores.
- It also revealed that 5% of consumers found errors that would have led them to pay significantly higher amounts for mortgages and loans.

Do not let any such errors on your report make you pay more than you should. Make sure you pull and carefully check the three reports, disputing any errors that would affect your score – such as wrong credit limit(s) or an incorrect account.

While the dispute process may not lead to instant results, but the effort and time invested into it would be worth it.

#3. Pay off any outstanding debts or delinquencies.

- Similarly, to lenders and underwriters of your mortgage will need some certainty that you are a trustable buyer who will be able to make payments on time.
- This means that having any delinquent accounts or outstanding on the credit report may hurt your chances. Before applying, try to clear any such accounts, and if that is not possible, make sure that the impact of late payments is minimized.
- You can do this by burying it with years of payments that have been made on time.

#4. Decrease the percentage of your income that goes into paying debts.

- Your debt-to-income ratio, or the part of your income that goes into paying debts, is a significant factor that your underwriter will take into consideration.
- This will help evaluate what credit risk you pose, and that amount of debt that you can safely handle. Studies are indicators of the fact that those who come with a high value of such ratio are likely to find it tougher to make regular monthly payments.

Lenders may not be able to trust you with money if you are already using a large part of your income to pay debts.

Lowering this ratio needs you to do either of the two – decreasing your debt payments or increasing your total income. While the latter may seem tough to do, there are quite a few options to do so.

A little increase in your income could be a great help in lowering this ratio.

#5. Beware of applying for credit.

- Since you need a credit score as high as it can be while applying for a mortgage, you should try to hold off on getting more credit, especially when your underwriter is trying to make a decision on your mortgage.
- Every credit application that you fill out in this time could lead to an inquiry that would significantly decrease your score.
- This is what makes it important to consider the impact of each application that you fill out for seeking credit in this period.

The only thing you should keep in mind is that improving credit score will not happen overnight – it is something that could take quite some time.

It is essential that you begin keeping your credit score in check the moment you start thinking of buying your home. There is no reason for you to pay more interest than you should – and keeping your credit score in check and at a good level is a good way to do so.

Keeping Your Credit Clean Before Purchasing a Home

When it comes to your credit and purchasing a home, you must be extremely careful with what you buy and the money you spend. A wrong move and you can wave goodbye to your new home.

There are many factors that come into play when it comes to keeping your credit clean before purchasing a home, which you will need to pay serious attention to during this process.

It's important to keep in mind that after you apply for a loan, or do anything which involves your credit score and report directly, all of the information is then documented in your current credit report.

In the case of purchasing a new home through an application for a mortgage, it's best to wait and take out any credit cards, and not apply for a car loan either.

Killing Your Debt to Income Ratio

Were you aware of the fact that messing with your income ratio when purchasing a home can bring negativity into the process? If not, then there are things that you will need to know.

For example, if you are attempting to take out a home loan, but are also purchasing a new car, your lender will evaluate all of your debt-to-income ratios, and make a decision based on that information.

Your ratio represents the amount you are spending on a monthly basis when it comes to making debt payments.

On a typical basis, mortgage lenders generally prefer a ratio to be no higher than 36 percent. If a loan comes up during the process of a home loan, such as a car loan, for example, your mortgage lender will probably get in touch with you to go over it, and may not approve the loan for the home.

Your Credit Report and Why it Matters

As previously stated, every loan you apply for, credit card you pay for, or anything in general that involves your credit, will show up on your credit report as an inquiry.

Lenders will look into your credit report to see whether or not they should grant your loan or not.

For example, if you are applying for too many loans, or have too much debt at the same time, your report will be negative to any lender if you are in the process of being considered for a new loan.

Paying Your Loan in Cash?

If you are going about buying a home with cash, without having to obtain a home loan, then you will be set.

This means that your credit report will not have the debt documented on it, unlike if you were to first take out a loan for your purchase.

For example, if you plan on buying a car and want to apply for a mortgage at the same time, you can do so by paying for your new car in cash. If you go this route, your mortgage lender not be aware of the changes on your credit score or report.

Although, your mortgage lender will be able to look into your bank account and see the balance you have, for any and all accounts that you have open.

Therefore, using a savings account to purchase anything large, such as a car, can impact your chances negatively when it comes to having any type of loan approved.

Totaling Your Monthly Costs Compared to Your Monthly Income

If you heard that you should do this before you apply for a loan, but are unsure of how to do so, follow the steps that are listed for you below:

1. Record all your gross pay for each month, before any deductions for your insurance, taxes, or anything applicable.
2. Multiply the number you up with by .28, which equals 28%

The amount that you come up with for the second point is the amount the majority lender will use for a guideline when it comes to your housing costs.

This will include property, homeowner's insurance, interest, principal, etc.

Tips to Be Prepared

When it comes to taking out a loan with a mortgage broker for a home, you are going to need to be armed and prepared to the tooth.

This means you're going to need to produce a lot documents, beginning with tax returns from years before.

Lenders will also want to see bank statements from a monthly basis, as well as proof of your income and all debts you may have.

It's also a good idea to have sources for any big deposits you may have ongoing.

If you have any family or friends making a down payments for you, you will need to have a written letter to documents such information for your lender, too.

You are also going to need quite a bit of money for multiple things, such as the down payment. You are also going to need funds for your closing costs, at least a year's worth of taxes, insurance payments, and some extra cash just in case.

Your mortgage lender will also want to ensure that you will have an adequate reserve.

This is just in case something in the home breaks down, something needs to be replaced, or if you lose your job and will have money to fall back on while you look for new employment. Multiple financial experts agree the general rule of thumb for a down payment is 20% however you can buy a home with as little as 3% down or 0% down if you are military personnel.

Keep in mind with less of a down payment, your monthly mortgage payment will be higher.

Anytime you put less than 20% down you will be paying monthly private mortgage insurance to the lender included in your payment.

Be Ready For Anything

In conclusion, it's never a good idea to apply for multiple loans at the same time, such as a mortgage or a car, especially if you are in the process of obtaining a mortgage.

If you need to make a big purchase while applying for a home loan, talk with your lender first because that purchase could disqualify you from your home loan then you lose out on your dream home.

Chapter 4
Programs for First-Time Home Buyers

Grants for First-Time Home Buyers

While looking for a home, you may find there are several grants and down payment assurance programs available for first time buyers. Your lender should be knowledgeable in this area and guide you and see if you are eligible for the local benefits in your area.

Be careful too, as there ae always people looking to take advantage of your situation. Matters involving money always needed to be handled with care.

Various programs and subsidies can help cover your down payment and/or closing costs when buying a home.

Grants can be as important as your home loan when buying a home if limited funds are an issue. Unlike a loan or debts, a grant does not need to be repaid. This means these programs are aligned to help future homeowners and possibly revitalize a community.

Grants are gifts of money usually from a non-profit entity and never have to be paid back.

There is no such thing as free money, and there are some requirements you'll need to meet, however a grant is as close as you can get to free money. The grant can cover a portion or all of your down payment and closing costs.

If you are buying a home for the first time, it is in your best interest to check with your lender to see if you are eligible for any of the grants to buy a home in your area. Your lender will help you qualify for the grant and complete all the necessary paperwork and requirements to get the grant funds.

Lack of down payment is one of the biggest challenges for home buyers, however if you can get a grant it will increase your chances of becoming a homeowner without having to wait years and years to save enough money.

According to the recent census bureau, 67% of American own their home, which means there is plenty of room left for the rest of the population to achieve the American dream of homeownership.

There are some steps to follow. First, find a grant in your area for homebuyers, Next, have your lender see if you are eligible for the grant. Finally complete all the necessary paperwork and requirements to get the grant funds.

HUD (Housing and Urban Development) has a great website has resources for buying a home, whether your first or tenth home. HUD website provides important information you need to help you on your journey to homeownership.

Different states have different programs and conditions for homebuyer grants. The one thing they all have in common is that all 50 states have grants for first-time home buyers.

Subsequently, many cities and counties have their own grant programs. Check with your community and your lender to see the availability in your area.

Buying your first home seems like a huge, expensive undertaking but you don't need to worry because help is available. Don't be afraid to ask your lender, your real estate agent, your friends, co-workers, etc because you never know what aid is out there until you ask.

Tax Credits and Tax Breaks for First-Time Home Buyers

Finding ways to accumulate extra cash and save money can appear elusive, but there are a number of tax breaks designed to make it easier for buyers to buy their first home.

Who can qualify for the Tax Credits?

As per the rules laid down by HUD (Housing and Urban Development), only an individual who meets these certain conditions can be considered a first-time home buyer.

- A person who hasn't owned a residence during a tenure of three years, up until the day they purchase the property
- The same rules applies to the person's spouse as well
- Any single parent who owned a home jointly with their former spouse during the time they were married
- Someone who has owned a property, that wasn't permanently affiliated to any foundation as per the proper regulations
- A person who owned a residence which didn't comply with the state or local building codes

Another important thing to note is the difference between tax credit and tax deduction. Often times people think these terms are essentially the same.

However, they are not. Tax deduction actually reduces your taxable income. In comparison, a tax credit is a reduction in the amount of taxes you owe to the government. You can save considerable amount of money with tax credits.

Tax Credit and Tax Break Program Options

#1. Mortgage payment interest deduction.

This deduction is fairly well known. Nevertheless, this is the one of the most beneficial tax breaks that home buyers cab take advantage of.

The mortgage interest deduction is valid for loans up to $1 million. It covers the interest paid on your mortgage loan. You are able to write off the mortgage interest you pay on your annual federal tax return to lessen the amount of taxes you owe.

Check with a tax professional to see how this will affect your personal situation.

#2. Mortgage Credit Certificates (MCC).

The mortgage credit certificate is another program that helps thousands of first-time home buyers obtain a tax break. The IRS stated that the program is aimed at helping the lower income groups afford their first home.

This program is different than the deduction program since it reduces the amount of taxes you owe.

Depending upon the price at which you purchased your home, you can get back up to 30% interest you pay as tax credit. Although the program isn't that popular, it can be helpful to first time buyers to help you get back a considerable portion of money every year.

It's important to note the program is administered by local authorities and can vary by which state you live in.

To qualify for the mortgage credit certificate program, you must get with a local lender who is qualified by a local entity to help you.

#3. IRA Withdrawals.

Getting ready to buy your first home? Don't overlook getting some money from your IRA if you have one. If you're a first-time buyer you are eligible take take out up to $10,000 from your IRA.

This money can be used for your down payment or closing costs and first-time homebuyers who draw from their own IRA, will not have to pay the 10% penalty applied for early withdrawal. However, you'll still have to pay regular income tax on the withdrawal.

Every individual is entitled to get a lump sum up to $10,000, even if it's from the IRA of family members.

* Check with your tax professional for more details.

#4. Home Improvements.

Home improvements can earn you tax deductions in multiple ways. You can use a home improvement loan to finance the cost of repairs and improvements in the home. These loans qualify for a tax deduction.

Interest on home improvement loan is deductible up to $100,000 in debt. When you decide to sell your home in the future you can add the improvement costs to the value of the property. If the selling price of your home is more than you spent to procure it, then the extra income will be considered taxable.

You can reduce this taxable income by adding the home improvement costs. This may help you save money in taxes when you decide to sell.

#5. Home Office Deduction.

Do you work from home? If you do, you're in for a treat.

The amount of space in your home that is dedicated to your work activities is tax deductible. This deduction will include loan, interest, insurance, utilities and repairs.

However, there are certain guidelines for taking advantage of this deduction.

* Check with your tax professional for more details.

#6. Home Energy Tax Credits.

The IRS rewards homeowners who make efforts to create eco-friendly homes that benefit the environment.

The Residential Energy Efficiency Property Credit can cover the costs spent towards making the home more efficient.

Homeowners can save 20-30% of the costs incurred for installing energy efficient appliances and upgrades.

Another factor is that the improvements you are doing to get a credit will also reduce your tax bill and possibly your utility bill.

To apply for this tax credit, you must invest in appliances that harness energy from renewable sources. Examples of these sources are solar panels, wind turbines, fuel cells, etc.

These are not the only tax programs, there are other programs and you'll want to explore these to make sure you get maximum benefit.

Chapter 5
14 Common Mistakes First Timers Make

Congratulations! You are considering investing and owning your own home rather than wasting your money on renting.

While you are it, it's imperative you avowing the following 14 mistakes first-time homebuyers usually make:

#1. Failing to Budget for a Home Loan.

Homeownership is a cheaper alternative to renting in the long run and it is a forced savings plan. However, in the beginning it can feel more expensive. This is especially true if you need to get a mortgage to purchase your dream home.

If you need to get a mortgage, remember that you will be making monthly payments to pay it down for a number of years.

Therefore, it is important to budget for your home loan beforehand. You need to determine whether your income can accommodate the added expense or not.

If you are unable to afford making the monthly mortgage payments on your home loan, it would be a mistake to try and own a home at this time.

#2. Ignoring Your Credit Score.

Your credit worthiness can be summarized by 3 digits called your FICO credit score. Those three numerals will draw the line between owning a home and renting.

Even if you have an impeccable sense of financial responsibility right now, your past credit can haunt you.

You could have a hard time getting a home loan if your past credit history shows problems with payments or if there are errors in your credit report.

If you go ahead and apply for a mortgage loan without checking your credit score, you could end up paying a lot more than you expected.

It's best to complete the credit check beforehand. This way, you will be prepared and avoid paying extra when you don't need to.

#3. Disregard Housing Market Trends.

Just like other financial markets, the housing market fluctuates from time to time. Sometimes it favors buyers, sometimes it favors sellers.

There are a number of factors that affect housing market trends. This includes the ratio between supply and demand, interest rates and the overall condition of the economy.

It is also imperative that you consider how the housing market changes in your ideal location. Home values vary from location to location.

If you disregard the market and trends you could buy a home and possibly overpay for that home. Knowledge is key, and your real estate professional should provide market trends so you can make informed decisions.

#4. Not Getting Pre-approved for a Home Loan.

Some people are so anxious to buy a home they actually go shop and buy a home before they find out if they can afford it.

If you have already started your house hunt, STOP, and go get pre-approved for a home loan. Without a pre-approval, sellers will not take you seriously and your offers may have a hard time getting accepted.

To avoid disappointment, it is important to get pre-approved for a home loan first then go home shopping. You'll know what you can afford and you'll have the pre-approval letter to provide to the seller so they know you are a serious buyer.

#5. Overlooking the Home Resale Value.

Another huge mistake you can make buying a home is not considering the fact that you may need to resell the home in the future.

There are a lot of things that could force you to sell, such as job transfer, job loss, financial problems, health issues, family matters, or wanting a bigger home in a better neighborhood.

When this happens, you might find the need to sell this house and hopefully for a profit. You never want to overlook the resale value of the home you are going to purchase. Ask your real estate professional for information and stats on the house.

Some of the questions you will need to ask yourself is: Will it be easy to sell this house? Will buyers be interested in buying it? Is it in a good neighborhood? Is it appealing? Will it sell for a profit in the future?

#6. Trusting an Unprepared Real Estate Professional, or having a Bad One.

Having a buying agent by your side is highly recommended and in most cases will not cost you anything for representation.

There are pros and cons of dealing with real estate professionals, however they can take a huge burden off your shoulders when it comes to looking at houses and finding the right house.

Also, remember the seller's agent represents the seller and the seller's goals. They may not be 100% truthful about the house.

If you trust them blindly, you may regret it later.

Make sure your agent represents you and has your best interest at heart.

#7. Settling on a Verbal Agreement.

Verbal agreements will not stand up in court so you shouldn't agree to anything verbally when buying a home. Proving that you verbally agreed or shook on it would be difficult to win so avoid it at all costs.

Everything you do needs to be in writing – period.

With all terms and conditions in writing it will avoid any miscommunications and you have something to present in court if the seller fails to keep their end of the deal.

#8. Disregarding Hidden Costs.

This is another common mistake first-timers make.

You need to have some funds set aside when buying a home, since things can happen and if you plan to complete the purchase it may require more money.

There are times additional inspections or repairs come up during the buying process that you didn't know about upfront.

Before signing anything, make sure you know what the expected out of pocket costs are and have a cushion set aside just in case an unexpected expense comes up.

#9. Ignoring the Home Inspection.

Don't rely on the seller and the agents to tell you the condition of home.

Get a home inspection.

Before you proceed with the purchase of the home, you should get a home inspection. The professional home inspector will go over the whole home and provide a detailed inspection with photos as to what the condition of the home is.

#10. Following your "Love at First Sight" Gut.

Not everyone or everything you fall in love with at first sight becomes your true love, right? A house may appear to be everything you ever dreamed of, but it might not live up to your expectations.

Before falling in love, check the home out thoroughly. Make sure it fits your needs and desires and especially your budget. Is it right for you and your family?

#11. Being Indecisive.

It's unwise to rush into purchasing a home but it equally silly to take too long to make up your mind. If you take too long another buyer could come and buy the home right out from under you and there goes your dream home.

Market trends change and by waiting you could find yourself paying more for the same home since you took too long to think about it.

#12. Relying on Online Services Only.

Many services are available online these days by a click of the mouse and most people have become too dependent upon them. It's true homes can be bought online, mortgages can be obtained online, but failure to establish a personal touch with the lender, the seller, the agent could present a huge and costly misunderstanding in the future.

This is the biggest financial decision you will make in your lifetime and you shouldn't rely completely on online vendors. With the right real estate professional, the right lender, you could have an amazing experience with the expertise of the professionals by your side to guide you every step of the way.

#13. Forgetting the Costs Associated with Owning a Home.

Just like a car, a car requires maintenance. Maintenance on your home requires money. You have to prepare for the costs of owning a home to keep it safe, secure and environmentally friendly. You also have to be ready for major or minor repairs as these may come up unexpectedly.

Ongoing costs such as property taxes, homeowners insurance and utilities need to be budgeted for as well.

#14. Entering Multiple Agreements.

While it's smart to do your comparison shopping of different homes before buying, you might end up with multiple accepted offers. This is especially true in hot markets where there is limited inventory or you are making multiple bids that you may not intend to honor.

Before entering any agreement, it's imperative you ensure you are ready to fulfill your end of the bargain and follow through.

If you can avoid the above mistakes commonly made by first-time homebuyers, you will have a smooth, successful transaction and avoid rookie moves.

Avoiding these mistakes can help you make the right choices when it comes to finding a home for you and your family that you can take pride in.

Searching for the Right Home

Buying a home is an exciting event and one of the biggest financial decisions you'll make in your lifetime and the process can be very daunting.

It's a major investment and must be taken seriously. It's not like buying a pair of shoes or a TV, because you can't just return it if you don't like it. Once you buy, you are in for the long haul as they say.

To avoid costly mistakes that could haunt you for years to come, you need to make sure you do your homework and due diligence while you're house hunting.

Viewing a Home

For most people, looking at homes is fun. It's tempting to think of this as the first step to buying a home however it's not.

Assuming you have your down payment, your mortgage approval, and other financial issues handled, the first thing you need to do before looking at homes is determine what you're looking for.

What is your criteria?

Do you need a set number of bedrooms and bathrooms?

Do you want or need a yard?

Do you want a property in a particular neighborhood or school district?

How much are you willing to spend?

Answering these questions will save you a lot of time and effort before running around looking at homes that don't fit your criteria.

Once you've decided on your criteria, call your real estate agent. Let them know what you're looking for and what your price range is.

He or she will get to work on your behalf finding the available properties that meet your criteria so you can start viewing these homes. Then the fun starts... finding that perfect dream home.

Schedule Adequate Time to View

When going to look at homes, make sure you set enough time aside to be able to view the homes on your list.

Schedule a few hours to really go over the house. Make notes, look over major things like plumbing, electrical, windows, doors, etc.

After which you've selected a home you'll need to schedule time for inspections and appraisals. You'll likely be living there for some time so it's best to invest time in the home now to make sure you don't buy a lemon.

Be Thorough

Be thorough when checking out your new prospective home. Open drawers, cabinets, cupboards, lift up rugs or carpet if necessary.

You are about to make a substantial investment and you want to know exactly what you're getting.

Sellers aren't obligated to tell you every little thing wrong with the home since they want top dollar so don't expect them to lay out the dirty laundry. That's why it's so important to get a home inspection to discover any hidden defects with the home. A creatively positioned chair could be hiding something, and you should look where you need to.

Of course, if you already hate the home from the beginning then don't bother with the time or money of inspections. However if this is a contender, then you need to do your research and look behind every door and open every closet.

What Comes With The Property?

Confirm what comes with the home at the time you make the offer to the sellers. For instance, do the appliances stay? Are the ceiling fans included? Window coverings? Make sure to get confirmation in writing exactly what comes with the home if you buy it.

Don't Be Fooled By Staging

Most sellers use staging to make a home look more appealing when they are selling it. Sometimes clever design tricks can draw attention away from a problem. Lighting can also distract your eyes from potential issues. Beware of fresh paint. Is it for an update or covering a potential mold or water damage problem.

While you are looking at the home try to look beyond the immediate aesthetics of the interior décor. Focus on what you will get, the bones of the home, when all the furniture is gone.

Keep Emotion Out

When initially looking at homes it's easy to get emotionally attached very quickly. Try to keep your emotions aside and look at it as a building that needs to be inspected.

If you get attached from the very beginning, it may sway your decisions and you could end up with a money pit and all sorts of problems because you let your emotions decide rather than logic.

View It Multiple Times

If you like a particular home, view it multiple times. You're more likely to identify any potential problems if you look at the property several times and at different times of the dy.

This way you'll see any inconsistencies with the home. You'll also be able to see what traffic may be in the area, such as school zones, bus routes, etc.

Consider Overall Context

When viewing a property don't just consider a property on its own, view it in the context of its' location.

What is the area like?

Is the property adjacent to a noisy intersection, freeway or train route?

Is there a commercial center nearby or a casino bar that may get noisy at night?

How close are you to things you may need such as the kids school, public transit, grocery store, urgent care or hospital?

All of these are legitimate questions to ponder when viewing properties, as some of these things can add or deter from the overall enjoyment of your home.

Let Your Real Estate Agent Do Their Job

We've already warned you NOT to go house hunting on your own, unrepresented. An unrepresented seller is also dangerous.

Apart from the fact that is isn't safe, it also makes you vulnerable. A seller's agent might think you're unrepresented and try to take advantage of you.

Let your agent do their job and if you happen to come across a property that you like that your agent didn't show you or maybe you found online, chances are it's not available and it doesn't meet your criteria.

If you like the look of that property, definitely call your agent with the address and that way they can see its availability and arrange for a showing.

Condition of the Property

When looking at the home, there are important things to look out for. Walk around the inside and outside of the home checking the stucco or siding, exterior and interior walls, and ceilings for any cracks. Hairline cracks are possibly expected in some locations. Cracks can be a sign the home is not structurally sound. Points at which extensions join are good places to look, as cracks will often appear there.

Look for loose or broken tiles on the roof or broken guttering, damage to the drywall and weaknesses of the floors.

Any signs of a problem anywhere on the structure of the home should be questioned from the seller as to what caused it.

How long has it been like that?

Will it be fixed?

Furniture or accessories like rugs could be hiding wall cracks or problems with the floor, so again, look under rugs, behind furniture or move things around if needed.

You might love the home, but if major cracks or any of the walls look like they are bowing it could be a sign of major issues or water damage. You may need a structural engineer to come in and take a look.

Watch Out for Mold

Mold is a major issue that could cost a lot to repair. Don't just look for it, use your nose and smell around. Mold has an odor and gives off a musty smell, even when there are no visible signs.

Plaster that is flaking, watermarks on the walls or ceilings, water stains, even a fresh coat of paint in a particular room or section of the home could cause a red flag and me be an indication of mold.

Don't forget to inspect the ceiling and around the floor boards for evidence or leaks or water damage.

Heating, A/C and Electrical

Other aspects to consider when looking at the general condition of the property are the heating and air conditioning systems.

Have an expert assess that they are appropriate models and capacity for the home and that they are in working order.

Check the fuse box, it shouldn't be old or outdated, must be easily accessible and in good working condition. Ensure wiring was done properly as you don't want to spend a fortune rewiring the home to bring it up to current day standards.

Check the power outlets to make sure they work and there is enough for your needs.

Basements and Attics

Also check the basement for evidence of mold or moisture problems. Is there water spots or leaking on the floor or around the foundation? There shouldn't be any cracks is the basement walls. If there are wood beams, there should be no evidence of dry rot.

Don't forget to check the attic for water problems or leaks that may have affected to roof or insulation, walls and ceiling. While you're looking you'll want to make sure the insulation is present in the attic and that is ample for keeping the home insulated.

Plumbing

Check the home's plumbing. Is the water pressure sufficient and strong enough? Exposed pipes should be insulated to prevent freezing and breaking. An exposed pipe is a recipe for a water disaster.

For health reasons, check if the pipes are lead or not since if they are you will want to replace them.

Check the location of the water heater and inspect it. Check for leaks and corrosion. If you see any of those issues, it may need to be replaced.

Exterior

Check the exterior of the home for water around the foundation that could indicate drainage issues.

The ground should slope away from the foundation so water doesn't pool where the foundation meets the wall. If there is a porch, does it sit on foundation or just soil? Is the porch or deck in good condition free of termites or beetles?

Check driveways and any walkways leading to the home for cracks or crumbling.

Check the siding or stucco to see if it looks in good shape.

Is the landscaping complete or well maintained? Does it have a sprinkler system? If so that should be checked to make sure it works and does what its' supposed to.

Property History

Ask your agent for more details about the home if you really like it.

How long has it been on the market?

What are the comparables?

Was it previously listed? Has there been any price adjustments?

What was it worth in the boom right before the market crashed?

You may also want other information about the property which generally can be found on public records.

Public records shows the name of the owner, original age of the home, mortgage history, parcel number, previous sales of the property, property deeds and judgements or liens filed against the seller. Information about how much the property taxes are and whether they are paid or in arrears will also be available in the records area.

You will also be able to see if there were permits obtained to make any improvements or additions to the home. These permits (or lack thereof) could complicate the sale of the property.

Do not skip this search because it reveals important information about the property that you should be interested in and could save you money in the long run.

You can get all of this from your real estate agent, which is another benefit of using an agent. They have resources and connections to get the information and data about the property for you so you are not wasting valuable time for something they can get fairly easily.

If you are not using a real estate agent, then the local title company may be able to help you.

Making Choices

Once you have completed your homework, it's time to make a decision on whether or not you are going to buy a home.

It is important to step back and evaluate all the information from viewing the home, it's condition and public records.

Some things to keep in mind:

- You may need to compromise on some of your wish list items. No home is perfect.

- No matter how good it seems, there may be a few things you'd like to change. If only it was facing the golf course, or it was in that other neighborhood you liked, or if it cost a little less.

- At the end of the da, you will need to decide which things are most important to you. If you prefer neighborhood over the house, look for another home in that community. Or maybe a condo instead of a townhouse.

- If financing is the issue, you may want to discuss with your lender if you can increase your buying power. This is only if you could afford it. There is no point getting into financial trouble just to get a certain home when more affordable ones will do just as well.

- Lower your expectations of the home. If the inspection revealed a few minor things, you could buy the home and do the repairs yourself.

- Use the problems of the home as your leverage to get the home for less money. If you chose this route, get a quote first for the cost of repairs so you are prepared going into the transaction.

- Don't estimate based upon what you "think" it will cost. If you allow the seller to get the estimate for the repairs it may be in his favor.

- Be prepared to walk away.

Again, this goes back to our earlier point about not getting emotionally attached to the home until you bought it and moved in. If at the end of the day you find out the compromise required is more than what you're prepared to make, walk away.

Working with your agent, if you have to walk away, you will find something else that you love.

Chapter 6
12 Steps To Buying Your Home

Buyer Step #1: Figuring out what you can afford

You know by now that the homebuying process is complex. Buyers often feel overwhelmed and get frustrated during the process.

So, before you go out shopping for that new dream home, consider if you can afford it. In other words, is it in your budget or not?

The actual cost of the home could end up more than the selling costs because of the added agent fees, closing costs and inspections needed.

Upon first glance, the home might seem affordable to you, however there are hidden expenses involved when buying and its best to discover them upfront otherwise you could face financial problems later.

You need to take a detailed look at what you can afford to determine your housing requirements. Your lender will help you establish your buying power so you can be in the best position possible when you begin your house hunt.

Buyer Step #2: Make sure you can get a mortgage

Buying a home is the largest financial decisions most of us make in our lifetimes and unless you can pay cash for the home it requires a mortgage.

Lenders are there to help you get pre-approved for a mortgage so you can see your buying power and how much the mortgage will cost you monthly and over the life of the loan. Some lenders will qualify you for more than you really can afford so be firm with your desired payment threshold.

Buying a home is super expensive and emotional. It requires careful thinking and decisions about your current financial situation and your expected financial future.

Make decisions solely on budget and try to control the emotional influence.

Buyer Step #3: Create your list of wants and needs

It's time to figure out what you need in a home and what you want in a home. This list can be quite extensive depending upon you and your budget. However, you'll need to figure out what you need and what you are willing to compromise on.

Your wants and needs play a huge role in your decision make because logic fights emotion and then you settle somewhere in between.

When writing down your wants and needs it might help to put a value on each item that is important to you and then while you are touring homes you can see which ones come out with the highest point score.

Buyer Step #4: House hunting

Your mortgage is pre-approved and your wants and needs list is done, now it's time to go house hunting to see what's available on the market.

Depending if it's a buyer's market or a seller's market could dictate how fast or slow you go look at homes and how fast or slow you make and offer on a home.

Try to keep your list within your budget so you aren't disappointed looking at homes you can't afford.

It is also suggested you look at all the options in your criteria so you can make an informed buying decision rather than an impulse decision.

Buyer Step #5: Location, Location, Location

One of the most important decisions most people choose when selecting a home is its location. You can always change things about a home inside or out but you cannot change its location.

Home is a place you're connected to not only physically but spiritually as well. Each person has different requirements for their home for themselves or the family.

Some people desire city life and the hustle and bustle where as some want the suburbs or the county for space and tranquility.

Look around and see if you can envision yourself and your family there. Does it feel right? Then go for it.

Buyer Step #6: Home design

Modern, Rustic, Traditional?

Do you have a favorite?

Each person envisions something different for their dream home. Everyone wants that perfect dream home. When you are house hunting, make sure it fits you and your personality.

Buyer Step #7: Contact a real estate agent

Searching on the internet for a home is easy, sort of, but it could lead to misrepresentation or scams.

Finding an agent is necessary when buying a home. Your agent can locate the home you want that fits your wants and needs criteria and set up the appointments to show them to you.

They will have knowledge about the market, the community so you can make sure it's the right home for you.

By contacting an agent, you may be able to get the home for less since they have negotiating skills and connections in the marketplace. Agents have data and resources that the regular consumer cannot access. They could assist you in your buying decisions since they will add the logic back in where you are pulled by emotion.

Agents have all kinds of options to show you and they can help you avoid pitfalls or scams.

Buyer Step #8: Making the offer to buy

The first step in buying a home is making the offer. This means proposing a price to the seller of what you are willing to pay for that home.

In the real estate world, oral agreements don't hold their weight or carry legal validity. This is again where your real estate agent will help you with the purchase offer.

Real estate agents use standard purchase contract forms from their real estate division that has the legal verbiage to protect you. They also have the required disclosures to keep you litigation free. They have forms the sellers need to sign and disclosures requiring a seller to be truthful about the condition of the property.

If you choose to work without an agent you could be exposing yourself to lawsuits. Real estate laws vary from state to state and they can change over time. Are you up to date on the current laws and latest housing information so you eliminate the potential of future lawsuit?

The offer must conform to local regulations and mention price and all terms and conditions governing the purchase of the property.

For example, if the seller agreed to help with closing costs, then it must be in writing and it must be in the offer.

After drafting and signing the offer, it is presented to the selling agent and seller for review. In some states, the purchase contracts are drafted by lawyers representing both parties.

The purchase contract, if accepted by all parties, is binding and is equivalent to a money agreement or deposit agreement. Therefore, that is why it is so important it covers all the details like a blue print.

Some other items in the purchase contract include: the physical address, the legal description, the parcel number, terms of the purchase (if paying cash or there is a mortgage), promise by the seller to convey a clear title to the buyer, target closing date, value of the earnest deposit, contingencies, surveys, inspections, the type of deed that will be conveyed, legal requirements, and a time that the offer will expire.

There are time contingencies relating to the home inspection, the mortgage and appraisal that need to be addressed. These contingencies mean that you will go ahead with the offer if the items are met during the contingency periods.

Buyer Step #9: Depositing money in escrow when you make an offer

When buying a home, it is expected for the buyer to put earnest money deposit into escrow to show the seller good faith they plan to follow through on the purchase.

The contract is binding and the earnest money tells all parties you plan to proceed.

Escrow is the period of time between when the property enters into contract and the time when the property is transferred into the name of the new owners.

The initial deposit (earnest money) is collected upfront and held at the title/escrow company or attorney. This money is applied to your future down payment and closing costs. The amount of the earnest money is decided upon when you make the offer to the seller.

The escrow agent is a neutral third party that is there to assist both sides without bias. They are included so that the different terms and clauses are upheld. The escrow agent facilitates the title insurance from seller to buyer and ensures the property is transferred to the buyer free of any liens.

The money collected from the buyer is held in escrow until the seller completes their obligations and the buyer finalizes their mortgage.

If for some reason the buyer and seller are not able to fulfill their obligations, then they must mutually agree on how to deal with the deposit.

Buyer Step #10: Negotiations with the seller

This is perhaps the toughest part of the home buying process since there may be a lot of back and forth. A real estate agent is really handy during this time.

You want to always strive for the winning bid during negotiations. It requires skill, market research and sometimes luck.

Once you find your dream home and you are ready to make an offer, you and your agent should be reviewing the comparables in the area to validate the asking price.

Comparables or comps are model match homes that have recently closed just like the home you are looking at.

Once you have researched the comps then you can make a reasonable offer on the home you want. It may be important to visit the other homes similar to do your own comparison to the one you'd like. If your target home has unique features then that has to be taken into consideration.

Your offer can evoke three possible responses from the seller. First, the seller may accept your offer as it was presented. Second, he may do a counter-offer asking for changes to your offer. Or third, he may reject the offer all together.

To deal with their response, you must have the proper data and comps and then decide what is the maximum you are willing to spend on the home depending upon budget. Your agent can guide you here. Now you'll need to see how badly you really want the home.

In a seller's market you could lose out on the home if your offer is too low. Remember homebuying is a negotiation and business transaction so don't approach it with personal sentiments.

If the price the seller wants is too high and the comps don't match what they're asking, then you must decide what to do – over pay or walk.

Buyer Step #11: Closing Process

This time has various names and is sometimes called closing, settlement or close of escrow but whichever it is called it is generally done electronically and online. These days most forms can be signed electronically however there are still forms needing a live signature. The closing process is meant to bring all parties together for the common goal.

During this time the title will be reviewed to ensure its free of liens, title insurance will be issued to the new buyer, property taxes will be paid to current. All the other items, such as the mortgage transfer, the closing costs, legal fees and adjustments will occur. The closing agent will review the documentation from all parties.

The closing process, although involved is brief. It involves the completion of the transaction to the agreed terms.

In most cases of closing, the buyer and seller never meet in person at the same setting. They commit themselves to completing the paperwork with the objective to transfer the property from seller to buyer.

While the buyer gets keys to their new home, the seller gets a check for the proceeds on the sale. The closing agent deducts any costs to pay their existing mortgage and fees connected to this transaction.

During the closing process, the deeds, loan documents and other paperwork are prepared, duly signed and submitted to the assessor office for recording.

Before the closing in complete its advisable the buyer does one last walk through of the home to make sure nothing was changed, moved or altered.

The outcome during closing is the buyer receives title to the property, the lender gets their paperwork executed in public records, and the seller gets their proceeds.

Buyer Step #12: It isn't yours yet

While all looks good and things seem to be going well, deals do fall apart at last minute. This could be due to multiple reasons including buyer financing, home condition or even seller issues.

If buyers know these pitfalls beforehand it would be easy to avoid them.

Here are some things that could happen:

- Making sure your financing is finalized. Loan issues kill real estate deals. It is imperative you handle all your mortgage related items early on. It's easy for buyers to get wrapped up in the offer process and ignore their mortgage items. Then once it is time to address the paperwork their loan application is declined.

- Communication. IF there are changes midstream, best to expose them early on so they can be addresses rather than shoved under the rug. Many times the situation can be fixed if its known early enough.

- Low appraisals. Depending upon the market sometimes the value the appraiser places on the property doesn't match what the seller wants or what you have offered. The lender is only lending to you based upon the home's value since it is the collateral used for your mortgage.

- Cloudy title issues come up from time to time. It is up to you, your agent and your lender to discover any potential issue that could be on the title of the home.

All these things need to be kept in mind by the homebuyer. If anything goes wrong, contingency measure should be taken and make corrections or seal the deal and close.

Chapter 7
To Hire a Real Estate Agent or Not To Hire a Real Estate Agent?

Find a good one.

One might ask, what is the difference between a real estate agent and a realtor? They are not the same and a real estate agent is not a Realtor.®

A Realtor® is one who is a member and authorized by the Realtor's Association on a national level – (NAR) National Association of Realtors - and is a member of the local Realtor® association in their area. A good agent will still follow all the same rules and virtues as a good realtor. It shouldn't make a difference to you but the agent may not have the same access to the MLS or inventory databases as the realtor.

As well as being an association member, agents must fulfill some other duties and care to clients:

- Ethical and moral behavior and treatment towards the client
- To uphold and maintain the standards of care for the Association

- Obey the rules and regulations of the state which they are licensed and serve
- Caring towards the client they represent

How do you hire a great agent?

Most people find their agent by a recommendation from a friend or family member or online, so making sure they are the best for the job is important.

Most agents you'll encounter deal with residential homes. They help people buy and sell homes in your area or state. A good agent will be informed about the current market and everything you need to know about the property.

You may need to ask the person who recommended them why did you like them or you may have to research them online to learn more. It's like an interview... This is the biggest financial decision you'll make in your lifetime and the agent you select matters.

During your interview process you'll want to make sure they are experienced, have access to homes in the area and more importantly that your personalities fit. You'll be spending significant time with them during the buying process so it'll make it smoother and more fun if you like each other.

Some things to ask yourself.

Do they have the qualities like ethical behavior, motivation, flexibility to help you achieve your homebuying goals? Are they available on your schedule? Do they have positive feedback from previous clients?

Some other things to ask may be how many homes they've closed this year? This could be a gauge of how much experience they have. No deals = no experience. If that's the case, they may be nice but without experience may not be able to help negotiate the best deal for you. At this point you may want to search for a more experienced agent.

Possibly a way to check on an agents' compatibility for you and helping you could be:

- Previous closed deals – do they have a portfolio?
- Working hours – availability
- Are they motivated and loyal?
- Designations or certificates obtained?

Interviewing a good agent.

After confirming they are legitimate and ethical it is important to list the good and the bad qualities of the agent. It will be helpful in making a final decision. If the agent meets the criteria and you feel in your gut that they are right for the job, then go forward.

Next, you'll want to arrange a meeting and see what contracts they may require upfront (if any) before you begin house hunting with them. These contracts protect your and their rights from violations of rules on the agent's part. It can also protect you if your needs are not met during the deal according to the contract.

Then it's time to begin with your home criteria and telling the agent what you'll need:

1- Number of bedrooms
2- Kitchen, bathrooms, parking, etc.
3- Location desired
4- The range of your budget

By giving this criteria to your agent they will be able to locate the perfect home just for you.

How to make your first offer the best.

By now you've viewed several homes, possibly went to builder communities, looked at various neighborhoods and found a home you're willing to pay for. Or maybe it was love at first sight! Either way it's now time to make the offer.

This may be the most stressful part of the process – price negotiations. You know how much you can spend, and now it's time to consider all the possibilities.

The offer step requires preparation and analysis which is why you should have an agent representing you through this process. The agent will check on the comparables for this property and present a CMA. A CMA is a basic mathematical analysis of the properties with like features that recently sold to find the value of your future home. It calculates the square footage, number of bedrooms, number of bathrooms, yard, pool, etc.

This model will give an idea of the average basic cost which is the start of your offer. Afterwards you'll evaluate components that may increase or decrease the homes' value. For example, you know the owners recently changed out all the plumbing in the house. Or the opposite, their plumbing is 40 years old and will break down any day.

Then your agent will research market trends: is the market going up or down? What are the future predictions telling us? Are more people buying or selling? Are they things happening (good or bad) nearby to affect future value?

All of these calculations and forecasts take some time but you will be better prepared to make the best offer, and having a professional by your side will help you make the best decision.

Your real estate agent or realtor will help with this process and its normal activities for them. It will help you decide in a few things. It will help you figure out how much you should offer and which factors may or may not be in your favor.

After you agree on the price and terms, your agent will send over the contract to the seller and his/her agent. The seller will either accept it, or present a counter-offer. Then negotiations will go back and forth until you reach a mutual agreement.

Once the agreement is met, you move into the escrow stage.

Remember all agreements no matter big or small must be in writing to be enforceable and it will become part of your purchase contract.

Negotiating Price: Which tactic to choose

The goal of negotiating is to buy the house for the amount you are willing to pay. Think of the highest bid you're willing to pay and don't offer any more.

You may want to know a few things on the seller and their motivation to sell as it could help with your offer and negotiations.

- Why are they selling?
- Do they have to move by a certain timeframe? Possibly for a job?
- Family situations forcing a sale?

Buyer's market versus a Seller's Market

A buyer's market occurs when the supply (available properties for sale) exceeds demand (the number of buyers seeking to purchase properties). If you're buying a home, a buyer's market is the ideal time to make your move. You might be able to buy a great home for a lower cost than you would in a seller's market.

In a buyer's market you have more possibilities to have a successful offer. You can make a less than reasonable offer, demand improvements, a better closing date or even ask for closing costs from the seller.

A seller's market occurs when demand exceeds supply or there are more buyers seeking to purchase properties than there are available homes on the market. This often leads to multiple buyers interested in a single property often resulting in bidding wars.

In a seller's market, you may have less leverage, as you are not the only one in line wanting to buy this home. Your offer may be successful if you offer what the seller is asking for. If not from you then the next person may be the winning bidder.

Depending upon market conditions this may help or hurt your offer stance.

It is vital to understand that both the buyer and seller may forget the final goal; to buy and sell a home. Sometimes parties get carried away in the battle of negotiating. Lock your eyes on the end result and at the same time be realistic in your expectations of the situation. The following tactics will hopefully keep you focused.

#1- Use the middleman

Your agent, duh. That's why you hired them right? Your agent will act on your behalf as the middleman to negotiate with the seller's agent.

Using the agent as the buffer and the expert will save you time. They may also have useful information concerning the sellers, their intentions, etc... which the other party didn't disclose to you directly.

#2- Playing good cop - bad cop

Like in the movies one should take one side, the other take the other side. Not to cause conflict but to get closer to the seller and gain an alliance.

This will let the seller know that you are working on the compromise and are aware of his intentions. You can work with your agent with this tactic as well.

#3- Wait for boss man/boss lady

Sometimes there are 3rd parties (attorney, lawyer, executor, courts, professional or friend) that needs to see and evaluate the offer and give their opinion of expertise. This may be a chance to lower the seller's counter offer and keep your position.

This process may prolong things and you may have to wait. You could use this to your advantage if you don't want to wait and make it known you are considering other properties.

#4- Be curious

Ask questions. I always say if you don't ask you don't get. By asking questions, you may find out valuable information from the seller. It may reveal things you didn't know before and reasons for the sale. Possibly it could be your priceless leverage.

#5- Consider a compromise

Stubbornness never got anyone anywhere so it may be time to consider a compromise. If you may lose the whole deal at one point or another during the transaction, then you should be ready to compromise and possibly give in during the negotiation.

Compromise means you agreed in the end but meeting halfway and feeling good about your decision.

#6- Focus on the main goal

The goal is to get the home, right? Yes.

Sometimes people get so caught up in the negotiating back and forth they lose sight. Don't get stuck in the details. It can make a good decision and the process turn sour. Make sure you agree on the details and main points though before proceeding.

How to avoid mistakes during the negotiation stage

Whether its your first home or 20th, mistakes in the negotiation stage can happen, we are all human. Mistakes can be avoided if you follow some of these practices when buying and selling homes.

1) **Be Nice**

No one likes rude or hurtful people.

Try not to offend the seller during your home tour. You may not like their décor or style but discussing their poor taste while on the tour with them present could hurt their feelings. And they may decide not to sell to you.

2) **Be Calm**

Don't act overzealous.

Emotions take a toll during this process but being over anxious affects everyone. Most specialists agree that if the seller sees your excitement, they may not accept your first offer. To avoid the counter offer and back and forth, you should play it cool, no matter how perfect the home is for you.

3) Think Like a Seller

Try taking a different look or perspective at the situation. Imagine its you who is selling this same home is 2, 5 or 10 years.

Will it be possible for you to sell in its current condition? Will it need repairs or updates? Does it lack basic features that the market deems essential?

4) Get Professional Help

Spending money on attorneys or real estate agents can be costly, thousands of dollars in most cases. Be cautious with the less expensive services. If they are significantly less expensive you'll want to discover why and what you'll be giving up by using them.

It may be an indication of their lack o professionalism and cause you losses in the future. Pick your team carefully.

Don't rely solely on yourself especially if this is your first time buying a home. Check with friends, family, go online… there are plenty of resources out there.

5) Don't expect a lower price after the inspection

Bid lower than you can afford and make your final offer with the most comfortable price you can afford.

Most homes need some type of repairs and the repairs will most likely not cost the seller millions to fix. But don't expect to renegotiate the price once you see the inspection report.

Consider however the repairs as a negotiating point to get the items fixed or money as a credit to fix it yourself. However, unless its major items that break the budget you should be prepared to move forward and close.

On a side note: if the inspection is completed within your due diligence timeframe and you don't like the items noted to be repaired or the repairs are too lofty, you can cancel your contract without repercussions.

6) Sign cautiously

Make sure you've read everything and know what you're getting into before signing on the dotted line. Once the contract is signed it's very difficult to make amendments to the contract and terms without having to renegotiate a whole new contract.

7) Don't forget future costs

Budgeting is essential during the purchase of a home and beyond.

You will have to make payments to the agent and/or attorney including but not limited to your down payment, closing costs, escrow payments, deposits, etc.

There are inspections, appraisals, etc.

You definitely need to summarize all of these costs and make sure its within your budget to buy the home and cover all the required costs.

What happens with multiple offers on the property?

In a seller's market you might encounter competition for the home you want to buy.

Sellers could be considering multiple offers at the same time, so your first offer should be your best. They will make their decision based upon the best offer they receive (or so you hope). They may choose one buyer and only send counter offers to them.

Generally you will never know. However you can be creative to make your offer stand out, other than price. Your real estate agent can assist you with this part and help you.

Of course having a pre-approval for a mortgage (if you need one) is a good start. This is a letter from your lender stating you meet the criteria to get a mortgage based upon your credit score, income, bank statements, etc. This shows everyone your ability to pay for the home you're making an offer on.

You may also want to let the seller know about the financial options you have as some mortgage conditions and programs are more attractive and may influence the seller.

Try to bid close to the seller's asking price. Lowballing may insult them and kill your offer.

Review the contingency list, as the fewer that you have will make your offer more attractive to the seller.

I'd recommend against removing a home inspection because if you do you will not discover an issues or repairs needed and the seller will not be liable if you uncover something later.

Sometimes a larger than requested good faith deposit and down payment shows your commitment to the seller and could title the balance to your favor.

Negotiations can be stressful and usually the most nail biting time of the process but don't fret, remember the seller wants to sell and you want to buy and with your agent by your side, and a little time and effort, you will have a successful outcome.

Chapter 8
What You Need to Know About Home Inspections

The house hunt is over – Phew!

You have visited the home, maybe a few times and seen it at its best.

Now begins the due diligence phase and it is when the home inspections are completed.

What if all that prettiness is deception and something is hiding under that glossy surface?

The issues here may be from termites, to mold to leaky pipes to cracked paint.

This is why before closing on the deal on your new home, you will need to make sure that a home inspection is completed. It will help to evaluate the house condition and let you sleep safely at night before and after the purchase.

Why do you need a home inspection?

Some buyers skip this important step, especially if the market is hot or for budget reasons. Some think it impedes on the successfulness of their offer. Home inspections cost money, take time but if issues are found they save money and headaches.

Generally speaking you need a home inspection to see exactly what you are buying and what to expect from the property in the future.

During this process the home inspection specialists will examine the house in order to define the condition and viability of all the necessary systems.

Don't mix up a home inspection and home appraisal as they are not the same. The home inspection will clarify the current state of the home not its' current value.

After the inspections, you will receive a report determining the state of the home and recommendations of repairs or future steps, future expert opinions if needed.

Inspections and Common Mistakes

There are different types of inspections you can obtain. General or residential inspections will give an evaluation of the house elements and systems.

The list below may be enhanced or some points may be excluded, however it will give you an idea of what should be examined.

- o Exterior (quality of water drainage, condition of outside elements: yard trees, pathways, fences, decks, stairs, cosmetic issues, etc.)

- o Structural elements (visible foundation and framing condition, structure's upright position, etc.)

- Roof (installation quality, visible damages, shingles, roof tiles, and gutters conditions, etc.)

- Plumbing system (looking for any leaks, checking the water pressure, faucets, showers, material and aging of the pipes, etc.)

- Electrical system (checking fuses, any visible wiring, its type and condition, safety issues, etc.)

- HAVC - heating, ventilation, and air conditioning (inspection of chimneys, vents, house insulation, ducting, etc., checking if all systems work properly)

- Laundry room (ventilation and dryer systems, search for possible leaks and potential fire hazards)

- Bathrooms (proper ventilation, leaks, water heater condition and other possible issues)

- Kitchen appliances (proper working devices and their correct installation)

- Fire safety (checking smoke detectors, fireplaces and stoves)

Pest inspection will determine the presence of wood boring inspects, different kinds of insects, molds and fungi.

You need to know how much damage a termite population can cause and what to expect if there is termites present.

In addition, you'll want to know if there is mold present. This can be found in wet basements and be a health hazard so it's important you do the inspection.

If you live in specific risk areas, it would be wise to order additional services, for example, earthquake, tornado, or flood inspection. The specialist will help you to estimate the resistance of the property during the natural disasters, if they have a high probability of occurring in your region.

Your inspector will most likely recommend that you ask for a second opinion and another inspection if he has any doubts or additional concerns.

Don't procrastinate and wait for the last moment to follow his advice as there has been situations where the closing had to be postponed because failure to deal with discovered issues from the inspection report in a timely manner.

When the problem appears so late in the transaction it may be hard to resolve during that time, especially if both the buyer and seller have a strong opinion about them.

Choosing the right inspector is key. You want someone who has loads of experience, is honest and has good reviews.

You can go online to search for one, however your real estate agent or lender can refer you to one that they have personally worked with and that has good ratings.

The inspector makes a conclusion regarding the scale of the problem if some items need service or replacement and if some issues are not yet full-blown but there is a good chance that they may need to be watched or addressed.

It is common to interview a couple of home inspectors to find out more about them and how many homes they have inspected. Experience matters in this area. Furthermore you want them to be equipped with the latest technology and gadgets.

A lot of buyers neglect to attend the home inspection and only review the final report, however I think that is a mistake. Seeing it on a paper is not the same as seeing it in person.

This is one of the first opportunities you have to fully take a tour around the home and see its actual appearance.

The second most common mistake is to go to the inspection and be too afraid to ask questions about things you see. Inspectors do their job and there may be things new to you, so just ask. Don't be intimidated asking for an explanation on anything you don't understand. You are the one paying for his work and you have the right to ask.

Another mistake buyers make is leaving the home without checking the utilities. They may be off but you should ask for them to be turned on for the inspection to make sure all things work, no leaks and that everything is connected properly.

If you buy a new home it will undergo an inspection as well, just a little differently. They usually call it a final walk-through. Believe it or not, new builds also have issues.

Buying a home is the biggest purchase in your life and its not the time to gamble with such a large amount at stake.

What to do after a home inspection

After receiving the home inspection report, there are two possible outcomes. In the best-case scenario everything is fine and no work is required.

The worst-case scenario requires minor repairs and possible price renegotiation with the seller. The awful scenario needs major repairs and you may need to ask the seller to fix it or cancel the transaction.

Unfortunately there is no standard template and unified step by step regulation regarding what to do if there are issues with the home. This is where your real estate agent and lender will guide you and with their expertise to help you come up with a solution.

A lot depends on what needs to be repaired, what contingencies remain and if the seller is willing. Your contract may have a limit or cap as to how much the seller will pay for repairs. Some cases people have agreed to buy the home "as-is" and the inspection was only for information purposes and to calculate the cost of repairs or renovation.

If the repairs found on the inspection report needed are minor and don't compromise safety you may want to leave them be and move forward.

On the other side, if the repairs are major or will affect you living there, safety, health or value of the home, then you would definitely want the seller to fix these at their expense.

Some of the common problems that should be considered include the roofing, plumbing and pipes, fixing leaks, new wiring for homes 30-50 plus years old.

When to back off

As the professionals say you should cancel the deal if you cannot buy the house you want in the condition you want for the money you want.

It is most likely that if you're in a buyer's market it may be difficult to back off.

In any case, some repairs are just not worth it and these include:

REAL ESTATE HACKS FIRST-TIME HOMEBUYERS SHOULD KNOW

- If the seller refuses to fix the problem or pay to get it fixed and its dangerous to your health and you cannot fix it, then it's time to back off
    - You don't want to endanger you or your family, no house is worth that
- It may depend on the problem but if it needs to be fixed but you can't afford it right now or its way too expensive then maybe its tome to back off
    - You don't want to live in a construction site all the time, right?
- If the issue is likely to cause a chain of other issues and problems and it's difficult to estimate the cost then it's time to back off
    - If you can't predict the total cost of repairs it may be cheaper to cancel and start the home search again

No house is worth the future anxiety and headache. You should consider all the pros and cons very carefully and listen to your real estate agent team's advice. They are usually more experienced and can go over all the advantages and disadvantages with you.

Also don't forget your gut instinct. If you think you can manage it then go for it but if there are doubts and uncertainty then listen to yourself. There are more homes out there and your perfect home is waiting for you.

Can Inspections affect the Value?

The short answer is yes but not really. As we were saying the role of the home inspection is to find out any issues with the home and protect you the buyer from inheriting major issues with the purchase. Home appraisal is the report that determines the value.

During the appraisal they determine market value of the home based on its size, number of rooms, bathrooms, land, territory, etc. The appraiser is interested in like homes as yours to get an idea of the current market value.

The home inspection focuses on the home's condition and the appraiser is concerned with value since the home is collateral for your mortgage.

The appraiser doesn't take the home inspection report into consideration unless there are significant issues to the eye and it causes a question. For example, tilted façade and moldy basements are highly noticeable and will be noted in the appraisal report, but squeaky doors and interior water pipes wont.

Some lenders require a home inspection and an appraisal and have specific requirements what is and is not allowed. A property that has an of the red flagged items will require those to be fixed before the lender will proceed.

Don't panic if the report has a laundry list of items, most homes do. Make sure to read the report and evaluate if you can live with these items. Some items will be minor and you can fix, some may be affixed later in the future if you do any renovations. At the end of the day, as long as you are ok with the items then go for it and buy that dream home.

Chapter 9
The Closing Process

10 Things to Know if You are Closing on a Home for the First Time

Your real estate agent helped you prepare the offer, the list of contingencies (items to be remedied after the inspections) have been satisfied, and the contract is fully executed (signed by both sides).

Anticipation is rising and although it's too early to schedule the movers just yet there are some tips you should know before you become a property owner. Some of these we have touched on before but maybe you skipped ahead...

#1. Open Escrow

One of the first steps to closing on your new home after the contract is signed is to open escrow. Your real estate agent will usually guide you and handle this for you.

Escrow, on the average, last about 30-45 days depending upon the property, area and complexity of the transaction. During that time, the title/escrow company (which is the neutral third party) takes care of the items for both buyer and seller. The escrow/title company will receive and hold your earnest money deposit into the escrow account.

There are costs to both buyer and seller for their services and range depending upon area. Your real estate agent and lender should be able to help you with an estimate of what you can expect these fees to cost.

#2. Lock-in Your Interest Rate

Your interest rate will need to be locked in before you can close. If you have a savvy lender they will already be monitoring the market for you and helping you with this decision. When you lock in the rate is up to you but if you time it right with the market it could help shave thousands of dollars of interest off your mortgage.

Interest rates change daily, sometimes more than once in a day. So it's super important your lender has a pulse on the market to watch this for you.

#3. Have a Home Inspection

Making sure the roof doesn't fly off the first day you move in seems important, right? Well, it's in your best interest to get a home inspection.

Specialists will check the heating, air conditioning systems, plumbing, electrical and all appliances to make sue everything is in working order. They will also check for mold growth and other possible environmental health threats caused by lead, fungus and asbestos. No need to mention the potential harm growing mold can cause and lead to possible major damage.

Beware - Just like any service there are good ones and there are bad ones.

Pick a home inspector not on price (although important) but on experience and recommendations. They could save you thousands of dollars uncovering existing issues.

Even new construction homes need an inspection since sometimes things slip through the cracks.

#4. Get a Pest Inspection

Hiring a licensed pest inspection company will check the property. They'll look to see if the home is contaminated by flies, mosquitos, cockroaches, fleas, rats, mice, bed bugs, termites, beetles, critters, carpenter bees, ants, and other types of pests. Eeeewww...I am getting the heeby geebies just writing this part.

There is no need to explain how much damage even a small number of termites can cause. These issues can lead to major problems and repairs in the future.

Presence of any kind of contamination is the subject of renegotiation of terms, or a reason to rethink the deal completely.

#5. Fixing all the issues completely

If the inspections revealed problems, you may want to ask the seller to fix these, ask the seller to lower the price or a combination of both.

Some inspectors may note the issue requires a deeper look or a second opinion with a specialist. If that is the case then it is highly recommended to follow their recommendations and get it looked at as soon as possible. You will need the cost to remedy it so you can make an informed decision.

#6. Ask for the Title Search and Get Title Insurance

The title company will perform a preliminary title search on the property to see what liens exist on the home. This report will show what liens the current seller has to pay off to transfer it to you free of liens. They look to see there are no legitimate claims from relatives, collectors, and the like.

Title insurance is the legal proof the home is clear from liens and you are good to go. The title insurance is purchased through the escrow process from the title company at the closing. If you are getting a mortgage the lender will help you with this part. You will not need to do anything extra at this stage.

#7. Get the Home Appraised

The home appraisal determines the market value of the home (your soon-to-be property).

The appraiser evaluates the property on several factors. These include geographic location, general condition, proximity to objects of interest, value of similar homes, the recent sales of the neighborhood and neighborhood growth and potential.

If you are getting a mortgage you will need an appraisal since the home is the collateral for the promissory note you will be signing. The lender will need to ensure the home is worth what you are trying to borrow. They will select a residential certified appraiser to do the job.

Imagine this scenario, you negotiated a deal with a seller and the appraisal comes in low. You now have to decide will the seller reduce the home to the appraised value or will you pay the difference. If it's a declining market or the neighborhood is deteriorating this could cause low values.

On the flip side you could have the home appraise for more than you agreed and voila you have built in equity.

#8. Setting a Time and date for the Closing

The closing can be held in any agreed location. For instance, the attorney's office, the lenders office, the title company, or with a mobile notary.

The closing usually takes about an hour for each side to complete.

They say if you are getting a mortgage it's less expensive to close later in the month. Because the lender collects pro-rated interest it adds to your closing costs each day you aren't closed. You may not be able to control the date and sometimes getting closed earlier than later alleviates added stress.

However, if you must close in the end of the month, schedule it between the 20th and 25th to allow for conditions, final paperwork or technical issues that could arise.

If you schedule a closing and miss it, there could be financial consequences. It could be additional closing costs, it could be a per day fee or a penalty for the delay.

#9. Be present at the Final Walk-Through

The final walk through is a last chance to see your future home before you take possession. It is usually scheduled 24 hours before the closing.

The property should be in good condition specified in your contract. Check for any changes after the inspections and check for repairs that should have been made. Make sure everything is in working order and if anything else is needed.

If there is an issue, the closing day may need to be moved. Or upon mutual agreement the repair costs submitted to escrow and handled at the closing. Either way do not skip this step as it is super important you get the home as you expect to avoid disappointment.

#10. Closing Day is Here

Now the escrow marathon is done and you have survived every challenge and obstacle, it is finally time to sign your closing paperwork and get keys to your new home.

First, you want to make sure you have all your paperwork organized. You won't need it at the signing table but you will need to keep it all together. I tell people to get a white carboard bankers' box from the office supply store and put everything in that box and label it. This includes the contract, the title search paperwork, the inspection reports, the lender paperwork, home appraisal, bank statements, checks written, notes and conversations taken, closing cost worksheets and anything else.

Depending upon which part of the country you are in may determine how many people are at the closing. This could be the seller, their attorney, your attorney, their representative, the real estate agents, the lender, the title company, the escrow officer, the notary, and you.

The purpose of the meeting is to sign all the final closing

documents. You could sign all or some of these:

- CD (Closing Disclosure): This document contains all the final numbers for your home loan and lists all the costs. It also shows your payment and terms along with how much is needed to close. By law (per TRID), you are supposed to receive this 3 days prior to closing on the home so you have had time to review it and be prepared.

- Promissory Note: This is the instrument that binds you to the mortgage terms and conditions as well as any penalties in case you are unable to pay or fulfill your obligation.

- Deed of Trust: This document is a security for the lender that they will get their money if you are unable to obey the terms of the promissory note.

- Certificate of Occupancy (New Homes): If you bought a new construction home this is needed to show the home is clear to move into.

If your team of experts are competent enough this won't be the first time you're seeing these documents. Do not sign anything that is unclear or different than what you've seen before.

Follow your gut and make sure you understand what you are signing.

Risks and Delays on Closing Day

Even well-planned closings can have hiccups and experience delays. Some things may not go as planned and sometimes mistakes can be made during the signing of documents.

There are a few examples of how this could happen. If you or the seller's financial status change or if you got married mid-process and changes your name. It's possible some of the repairs weren't finished or one of you simply backs out of the deal completely. Anything is possible and you need to be prepared for every option.

If either of you refuse to sign the final papers because you changed your mind or found a better option the other party has the right to collect the damage fees or keep your earnest money deposit. This clause is in your contract and obligatory in all the agreements.

Closing is a big responsibility and financial risk for all parties involved. It is important to know that especially if it's your first time. You are at the home stretch and the home is almost yours.

Make sure to keep focused and keep all your paperwork together. It's a good idea to follow your attorney's, inspectors', lender and real estate agent's advice. They are your team there to help you have a smooth, successful closing.

Now breathe…

After Signing the Closing Paperwork

Once the home is officially in your name you get the keys. You are the official owner if record and now responsible for the home and the mortgage.

Closing on your first home is such a great feeling but comes with great responsibility. Nothing can be compared to buying your first home.

After moving in you can relax and enjoy your new home.

Hopefully these steps will help the first-time homebuyer be able to handle this incredible process will less stress and more knowledge.

Chapter 10
Moving Tips

Moving tips for the first- time homebuyer

Aside from buying the home and closing, I think moving is one of the more stressful things anyone can go through.

Whether the move is across country or within the same city or area, it always requires careful planning. From sorting to packing, labeling, unpacking and arranging all your items in your new home, it involves a lot of work.

This usually calls for additional hands to help with the tasks that need to be done. With a bit of help and resources the cost and stress can be minimized.

As with most tasks, organization and careful planning is key to moving. A checklist will help you remain organized and systematized with the task of sorting, labeling and packing your things.

Preparing the Checklist

Moving your entire home means a couple of checklists. You will want a list of tasks that need to be completed to keep you on track and a separate checklist for the contents/boxes in each room. You may also want to number the boxes as this will make it easier to sort and identify things while you're moving.

No task is too small for the checklists, since it pays to be prepared.

To help out here is a sample list that you can refer to. You should divide it into segments of time to keep you organized.

One Month before the Big Move

- Ask friends and relatives for referral to moving companies and inquire about their services and prices.
- Try to get at least 3 estimates for comparison so you can choose one that best fits your budget.
- Have a garage sale. If you no longer use it why not donate it or try to sell it. Less is more, remember?
- Go through your stuff and donate any unwanted furniture or clothes to charity.
- Gather up any financials your lender may need for your mortgage before you box everything up.
- Keep a file of all of your moving documents, such as bills, invoices, insurance, etc.
- Notify the utility companies of your move date so they can disconnect when you leave) for instance: water, power, gas, trash, sewer, cable, tv, internet, phone, etc.).
- Also set an activation date for the utilities at your new property so these are transferred to your new address upon moving in. Some of these services may require a technician or worker to establish the service so planning in advance is key.

Three Weeks before the Big Move

- Bring out the boxes and start packing the things you will not need in the coming weeks.
- Be sure to label the boxes with the room it belongs to so it makes your unpacking systematic.
- Did you finalize the movers? Or are you doing it yourself?
- Tell friends and family you'll be moving in a few weeks – maybe you can get some extra help.
- Request a change of address kit from the post office. Most of that is done online these days but you can go to the local post office to do it if you'd like.

Two Weeks before the Big Move

- Clean the room as you pack it to help facilitate the move. Then you won't be going back into the rooms over and over to complete the tasks.
- Set donation items aside and schedule a pick up. Salvation Army and other organizations will pick up your unwanted items.
- Request for time off at work as you will need it to sign your final papers and move.
- Prepare a suitcase with some clothes and things in it to use when you move so you will not have to dig in the boxes for clothes to return to work.
- Check the new home to make sure its ready for moving day. Electricity is on? Keys available?
- Throw out any un-needed and unusable items, especially flammable things and chemicals or left-over paint.

One Week before the Big Move

- ❏ If you have hired movers, call the confirm the date and time. Confirm the arrival and pick up so you can be ready.
- ❏ Draw up a time table for moving day. Arrival of the movers, time to pack up, lunch break, and time to unpack. This will give you a sense of what to expect on the day itself.
- ❏ With the help of family and friends, finish packing everything except the everyday essentials. The more things that are packed in advance the smoother the move will be.
- ❏ Make sure all the boxes are labeled on the side and top.
- ❏ Clean out the refrigerator and get rid of things that you aren't taking. Get a cooler ready for the things you will be taking. You can pack those on the morning of the move so they can be kept cool for moving day.
- ❏ Prepare several post-it notes with your phone number and new address for the movers and the help so everyone knows where they are going.

Moving Day is Here

- ❏ Pack a snack bag for today. It's a bid day and you need to pack lots of snacks and water to stay hydrated and sustain your energy.
- ❏ Zip up your suitcase for your transition.
- ❏ Pack up the bedding and disassemble the beds in the house.
- ❏ Have a meeting with the movers to make sure everyone is on the same page. You need to direct them on how you want things done and where things will go. Make sure if there are fragile items it is pointed out and noted to avoid breaking things.
- ❏ Distribute your post-it notes to the movers and help so everyone knows where to go.
- ❏ Double check every room in the house to make sure its empty and loaded into the moving truck.
- ❏ Do a walk through of your old home to make sure you haven't forgotten anything.
- ❏ Clean out the refrigerator.

- ☐ Inspect the new home, make sure you have water and power.
- ☐ Direct the movers where boxes and furniture goes.
- ☐ Set up your bed while you have the extra help.

Choosing and Hiring Movers

The checklist is pretty thorough with the weekly tasks you can check off as you go and items you can organize.

However a big factor to consider whether to hire movers is budget and time. Are they cost effective and will they save you time and headaches? Movers are a huge help with all the big items and with transport, loading and unloading over a short or long distance.

If you have large, pieces, delicate furniture or antiques, then hiring movers will be a practical choice. Choosing the right company is important and here are some things to consider:

1. Reputation. Ask around, from your friends and family even your real estate agent. You will want to select someone based upon experience. Have a few companies selected before you make a final decision.
2. Try to choose local. Oftentimes local is less expensive and more flexible. They may not be able to move you across country though, so check first.
3. Ask for an estimate. Let them come to your home, see how much stuff you have and where you're moving to so they can give an accurate estimate.
4. Read the contract and the fine print. Check their paperwork for hidden costs, insurance coverage, payment terms, their policy on damages, etc. Compare these to the other movers you've talked with and are considering to make your comparisons.

Cheaper isn't always better. The least expensive mover will not guarantee you'll save money in the end.

Less expensive could mean mediocre service or added services you weren't prepared for and that may bring unwanted problems along the way. You've heard the stories, right? Things being lost, precious items broker, moving trucks never showing up...

Choose wisely and take the precautions we mentioned before you jump in and pick the first mover you find.

DIY: Renting a Truck and doing it Yourself

U-Haul is the most popular in DIY moving trucks so its likely that if you choose to do it yourself, you'll be renting a U-Haul.

In this case you will be packing, loading, unloading and driving all yourself. This may be a great way to save on moving costs but only of you have a manageable amount of things to move.

You can call your friends and family for help in the packing and loading of the U-Haul which will save you money if you have help. This will not however save you any time, as it is a lot more to coordinate and you will be doing the hard work in addition to everything else.

If you want to get the best U-Haul deal and have a successful DIY move, here are some things to consider.

1. Time the move. Mid-week and mid-month are usually the least expensive times to get a better price since movers say the weekends and month-ends are the busiest times for them.
2. Look for cheap boxes to use for your packing. Used and recycled boxes are cheaper or sometimes free. Look behind grocery stores and ask your friends, there are boxes around when you least expect it.
3. Start packing way in advance. Don't do a last-minute stunt because you have your own truck rented. Planning ahead will minimize stress and help for a smooth move.
4. Organize your moving team. You will need all the help you can get from the packing, labeling and loading and unloading. You

won't be able to do it all on your own so you might as well ask for help early on.
5. Time the departure from your old place. Make sure you can get to your new home before it gets dark to make it easier for unloading. You may want to plan rests and meals stops so you don't wear out.

If you decide on DIY rental truck then you'll want to make a specific time table. Include things that you'll doing in preparation for your move. You may want to ask advice from people you know or someone who just did a DIY move. Their moving experience will provide you with tips on what to avoid and areas of preparation you may have overlooked.

Whether you make your big move with professional movers or do it yourself with family and friends, preparation and organization is key. You could hire the best movers there are but without preparation it will be stressful.

Your personal involvement in the planning and organizing is key and is needed to keep track of everything that needs to be monitored and accomplished.

Chapter 11
Horror Stories in Real Estate

You've seen scary stories on TV, perhaps heard about them from neighbors or co-workers, but you still haven't witnessed or experienced it yourself. Be warned – the first time is one too many.

Now that you're in the market to buy your first home, or maybe a second or third, congratulations!

Buying a new home is one of the biggest achievements in life for many people. Unfortunately, homebuyers – especially first time homebuyers – are the victim of horror stories.

There is a reason they say knowledge is power and its to avoid situations like these. I have been in this business over 20 years and still today hear about horror stories happening to good people.

Complete horror!

Here's a few examples of what I mean:

Lender Issues

REAL ESTATE HACKS FIRST-TIME HOMEBUYERS SHOULD KNOW

Alex was super excited about making her first home purchase back in 2012. Being in the Washington D.C. area she was limited to pricing options with many of the lower cost homes being over $250,000.

She went to several banks and got pre-approved for different amounts and different interest rates. She found her dream condo, made the offer and decided to go with the lender that offered the lowest rate of 4% – Bank of America.

She completed all her paperwork and submitted it with her 10% deposit. The interest rate wasn't the only factor as so far the people were super friendly, great at communicating, and made her comfortable with the process – until now.

Now all of a sudden it seemed as though Bank of America dropped off the face of the map when she needed them most. A closing process that should of taken 30 days or less turned into several months of waiting and BofA asking for an additional deposit of $20,000!

The ran her in circles and circles, dodged calls, told her excuses until the seller finally told her through her real estate agent that the deal was over if she didn't find another solution. Luckily the real estate agent referred her to her lender partner who was able to help her obtain another loan – although at 4.25% - much more quickly.

What became of Bank of America? Strangely, one of Alex's friends didn't have any problems and was able to finance her home purchase with them and move in all while Alex was having loan process nightmare.

I guess her friend was lucky, but Alex will never forget that horrible experience. It's a good idea to shop lenders to make sure you are getting the best deal but the lowest interest rate isn't always the best deal. Cheaper isn't always better.

A home loan is unique like you and I and it takes an experienced professional to be able to help you find the best mortgage to fit your needs. It is the biggest debt you are creating and it's important we help you manage that debt. It is also important that person helps and guides you along the way while keeping you informed and communicating with you. Seeing how they can help you goes a long way.

Bug Check

Have you ever heard of termites? They are bugs that eat wood and can eat away at the very structure of a home.

Ron and Jenna were happily married and planning on upgrading and buying their second new home. After a long search they found it – so they thought. A super bright, large kitchen, open living and dining rooms, three bathrooms, high ceilings, a fireplace and even a covered porch that made the home seem absolutely perfect for them.

They were especially thrilled about the price of $135,000. That kind of a price is a steal for what they were getting. They signed the contract and closed about 45 days later.

In less than 6 months later, the horrors began to unfold. Jenna was cleaning one of the bathrooms and she noticed tiny little ants with wings. Following Ron's advice she called the exterminator. When he arrived he delivered the first blow – the winged ants are actually termites.

The exterminator went under the house to assess the damage. Not only did he find the floor under the bathroom was completely infested, he also found termites at the other two bathrooms and spreading to more of the house.

The grand total of this problem came to over $12,000. This is an incredible amount of money to unexpectedly invest in a home that you've only lived in for less than 6 months.

How was that even possible, you ask?

REAL ESTATE HACKS FIRST-TIME HOMEBUYERS SHOULD KNOW

The key is to get to know the house you are buying. You should always hire the proper inspectors for your area or investigate on your own, especially for termites.

The initial cost of the inspections are worth it – a small price to pay - given the large investment you plan to make to buy the home.

Wedding Present

The stories can continue through an endless list.

I recently met a lady – we'll call her Sue – at a café recently with an intense first time homebuyers story. I happened to overhear her conversation so I decided to step in and ask her about it.

Sue and her fiancé were searching for their first home with the intention to buy it and move in before they got married. They had been told about a really great real estate agent in the city that they wanted to call home so they looked him up and asked for his help in finding the right home.

The problem was that the only praise they heard about this real estate agent was from the clients who hired him to help sell their home, not from homebuyers looking to buy a home.

He met with Sue and her fiancé to go over different homes he had on his list and then it was time to take a trip around town to see them.

There was one home in particular that he talked about profusely so they went to take a look.

While they did have a limited budget, Sue and her fiancé know what good quality was and they noticed right away this home had some problems. The basement doorway was weak, the upstairs bathroom floor bounced and all the light switches in the hallway seemed to pop and flicker. Although it was nicely painted the home didn't fool them one bit.

When confronted with these concerns the agent said these items could all be fixed later.

Although their gut told them not to move forward with purchasing this home, they agreed to a $10,000 price reduction and took the house.

Big Mistake!

The problems they had noticed went much deeper. The weak basement door translated into unfortified walls leading downstairs. The bouncy bathroom floor had been wet under the linoleum and about three inches up two of the walls.

The flickering light switches were warning them of the outdated wiring which had to be replaced. In the end, their $10,000 savings only helped to give them a bit of consolation when they paid their $27,000 bill for all of the remodeling.

Snake Den

The five bedroom house sat on pastoral acreage in the American countryside. At less than $180,000, it seemed like a steal… but it surely was no bargain.

Ben and Amber soon realized the dream home they had purchased in Idaho for their growing family was infested with hundreds of garter snakes.

Thousands of reptiles crawled beneath the home and in the outer walls. At night they laid awake and said they could hear slithering inside the walls. It was like living in a horror movie.

The home was likely built on a winter snake den or hibernaculum where reptiles gather in large numbers to hibernate. In spring and summer the snakes fan out across south east Idaho but as the days get shorter and cooler they return to the den.

The family would eat out a lot because their well water carried the foul musk smell snakes release as a warning to predators.

Each day before pregnant Amber and their two small boys got out of bed, her husband would a morning sweep through the entire house to make sure none of the snakes got inside. That didn't always work and one day he heard a scream from the laundry room where Amber almost stepped on a snake.

At the height of the infestation, Ben said he killed 42 snakes in one day before he decided he couldn't take it anymore. The war against the snakes was over – they lost.

He and his wife had little recourse when they decided to flee the home. They signed a document when they purchased the home noting the snake infestation. They said they had been assured by their agent that the snakes were just a story invented by the previous owners to leave their mortgage behind.

They were forced to leave the home, it was not saleable. They had to file bankruptcy and the home was foreclosed. They left the home right after their daughter was born, just within 3 months of moving in. They said the situation was so stressful that they felt like their lives were falling apart.

Several months ago the property briefly went back on the market. Now owned by the bank, it was listed for $114,000 a year later. The property has since been taken off the market, while the bank decides what to do with it.

Some homes on the market can seem too good to be true. In that story it sounds like they had good intentions to provide a home for their growing family. However they didn't have the proper inspections before going forward. Did the agent care enough for their well-being or just selling the home?

They we fed a story and they felt it was truthful, yet it cost them financially and emotionally. It can be tricky sometimes to tell if the agent is being truthful or not. If you aren't acting out of desperation, you will usually be able to see how they act, what they say and watch their body language. Sometimes your gut will guide you and you should follow it.

Lesson here… get your inspections done regardless what they say or tell you.

Homebuyer Plagues

Although the home inspector passed the home for Justin and Kate, there were still problems. For instance, the previous homeowner supposedly installed and tested a sump pump in the basement and it failed shortly after move in – flooding the basement.

The sunroom was filled with termites, costing the couple over $2,000 in repairs. After the termites were eradicated, they discovered the sunroom was covered in mold and there were no moisture barriers or caulking keeping moisture out.

A more experienced home inspector would have been able to detect the termites and the mold. The signs were there. The sump pump should have also been double check by the inspector and could have failed after the inspection.

Sump pumps can burn out, lose power, become clogged, or misaligned or malfunction in a variety of other ways. It is valuable to have a warning device installed that will signal water build up. These alarms can alert homeowners or neighbors of flooding so it can be resolved before water damage or flooding occurs.

Be careful, be smart.

REAL ESTATE HACKS FIRST-TIME HOMEBUYERS SHOULD KNOW

These horror stories are just a few but are certainly real situations that are happening every day. Do your homework before jumping feet first. It may take a little more effort or a little more time, but it's better to protect yourself against the biggest investment you will be making.

Too many people spend more time researching going on a vacation or buying a car than they do buying a home. You have time to educate yourself, ask for help, and go to your resources so you are prepared and equipped with knowledge when you are ready to buy your first home.

I hope these tips and hacks have helped you and give you information to put you in the right direction.

What will it take you to get in to your Dream Home?

Go to my website to find out more!

www.AundreaBeach.com

The information I provide is 100% free to you with no obligation. You can go to my website to get the free guides and resources I have.

If you want a discovery call or consultation, submit your information and we can have a conversation!

I'd love to help you buy your first home!

All My Best,

Aundrea

ABOUT THE AUTHOR

Aundrea Beach-Greco is a 22-year Mortgage Expert and holds the elite designation of Certified Mortgage Planning Specialist (CMPS) of which only 1% of Loan Officers in the nation have achieved.

For over two decades she has been blessed helping clients with the biggest investment of their lifetime – their home. She is committed to supporting her clients with accurate knowledge and information that will help them make strategic choices to meet their short and long-term goals.

This book was written to help first-time homebuyers avoid the common mistakes when buying their first home. Aundrea has laid an effective guide for first timers to navigate the home buying process. She believes in empowering her clients so they can make informed decisions and build and protect wealth through homeownership.

www.AundreaBeach.com